# Bible reflections
## for older people

BRF
Ministries

 Ministries

15 The Chambers, Vineyard
Abingdon OX14 3FE
+44 (0)1865 319700 | brf.org.uk

Bible Reading Fellowship is a charity (233280)
and company limited by guarantee (301324),
registered in England and Wales

ISBN 978 1 80039 304 2
All rights reserved

**Acknowledgements**
Scripture quotations marked with the following abbreviations are taken from the version shown. Where no abbreviation is given, the quotation is taken from the same version as the headline reference. NLT: The Holy Bible, New Living Translation, copyright © 1996, 2004, 2007, 2013. Used by permission of Tyndale House Publishers, Inc., Carol Stream, Illinois 60188. All rights reserved. AMP: The Amplified® Bible (AMP), Copyright © 2015 by The Lockman Foundation. Used by permission. www.Lockman.org. CEV: the Contemporary English Version. New Testament © American Bible Society 1991, 1992, 1995. Old Testament © American Bible Society 1995. Anglicisations © British & Foreign Bible Society 1996. Used by permission. GNT: the Good News Bible published by The Bible Societies/HarperCollins Publishers Ltd, UK © American Bible Society 1966, 1971, 1976, 1992, used with permission. KJV: The Authorised Version of the Bible (The King James Bible), the rights in which are vested in the Crown, are reproduced by permission of the Crown's Patentee, Cambridge University Press. MSG: *The Message*, copyright © 1993, 1994, 1995, 1996, 2000, 2001, 2002 by Eugene H. Peterson. Used by permission of NavPress. All rights reserved. Represented by Tyndale House Publishers, Inc. NIV: The Holy Bible, New International Version, Anglicised edition, copyright © 1979, 1984, 2011 by Biblica. Used by permission of Hodder & Stoughton Publishers, a Hachette UK company. All rights reserved. 'NIV' is a registered trademark of Biblica. UK trademark number 1448790. NKJV: the New King James Version®. Copyright © 1982 by Thomas Nelson. Used by permission. All rights reserved.

Every effort has been made to trace and contact copyright owners for material used in this resource. We apologise for any inadvertent omissions or errors, and would ask those concerned to contact us so that full acknowledgement can be made in the future.

A catalogue record for this book is available from the British Library

Printed and bound in the UK by Zenith Media NP4 0DQ

# Contents

About the writers ................................................................ 4

From the Editor ................................................................. 5

Using these reflections .................................................... 6

**Jesus stood up** Ro Willoughby ................................... 7

**Jeremiah's journal** Martyn Payne ........................... 18

**The Gift of Years** Debbie Thrower ........................... 29

**In hope and trust** Lin Ball ...................................... 38

**Fun and games** Derek Morgan ................................ 48

# About the writers

**Ro Willoughby** has been writing and editing Christian resources for many years. Licensed as a lay minister at St Chad's Woodseats in Sheffield, she is engaged in ministry with people of all ages. It is a great joy that she now lives close to her children and grandchildren!

**Martyn Payne** worked with BRF Ministries for 15 years before his retirement at the end of 2017. He has a background in Bible storytelling and leading all-age worship, and is passionate about the blessing that comes when generations explore faith together. For the past four years he has been the volunteer prayer advocate for BRF Ministries.

**Lin Ball's** career began in journalism over 40 years ago. She delights in the variety of work that's come her way: ghost written books, magazine articles about missionary work, communications for Christian charities and radio interviews on disability. Lin lives in the East Midlands, where she still writes, is active in eco-groups in her market town and enjoys long walks.

**Derek Morgan** is a retired IT professional having spent over 30 years in software development roles. A Christian for over 40 years, he knows his gifting will never be as a preacher or evangelist but his God-given passion is facilitating those who are! You will always find him somewhere in church using his gifts in technical, practical, musical and IT activities. He lives on the south coast of England.

# From the Editor

Welcome!

I still have some of my dear mum's leather gloves, including a beautiful purple pair she bought for our last trip away, to the Christmas markets in Vienna. Soft and pliable, unworn for over a decade, they hold the imprint of her arthritic fingers.

A few days ago, I took a pair of my own gloves from a coat pocket and was startled to see uncannily similar distortions. I inherited many wonderful things from my mum but arthritic fingers weren't her best gift. Three joint replacements and a small square of rubber grip cloth in every pocket, bag and drawer help me function, but my hands seem much older than the rest of me and I miss their strength and grace.

In his moving meditation on hands (page 35), Robert Glenny writes:

*Isaiah 49:16 talks of God's hands: God says to Israel: 'See, I have inscribed you on the palms of my hands.' Earlier in the chapter, we read 'the Lord called me before I was born' (v. 1). You were known, before you were capable of knowledge. There was no time when God's love for you was not etched into his very being. God knows you like the back of his hand.*

'It fits like a glove!' we say, when a fit feels precise and personal. To look at my gloves and see such a tangible reminder of my mother's imprint on my being is poignant and powerful, a faint reflection of the eternal imprint of our loving God on each one of us.

Go well

*Eley*
x

# Using these reflections

Perhaps you have always had a special time each day for reading the Bible and praying. But now, as you grow older, you are finding it more difficult to keep to a regular pattern or find it harder to concentrate. Or, maybe you've never done this before. Whatever your situation, these Bible reflections aim to help you take a few moments to read God's Word and pray whenever you have time or feel that would be helpful.

## When to read them

You might use these Bible reflections in the morning or last thing at night, but they work at any time of day. There are 40 reflections here, grouped around four themes, by four different writers. Each one includes some verses from the Bible, a reflection to help you in your own thinking about God, and a prayer suggestion. The reflections aren't dated, so it doesn't matter if you don't want to read every day. The Bible verses are printed, but you might prefer to follow them in your own Bible.

## How to read them

- **Take time** to quieten yourself, becoming aware of God's presence, asking him to speak to you through the Bible and the reflection.

- **Read** the Bible verses and the reflection:
  - What do you especially like or find helpful in these verses?
  - What might God be saying to you through this reading?
  - Is there something to pray about or thank God for?

- **Pray**. Each reflection includes a prayer suggestion. You might like to pray for yourself or take the opportunity to think about and pray for others.

# Jesus stood up

## Ro Willoughby

Have you ever been to a Proms concert at the Royal Albert Hall in London? Just before the concert begins, concert-goers in the ground floor Arena are instructed to stand-up. They remain standing throughout the performance. At the end, the audience usually joins them, rising to their feet in appreciation to give what we call 'a standing ovation'.

We stand for all sorts of reasons, not just to begin walking. We stand in queues waiting for a bus. We stand up to welcome a newcomer entering a room. We stand to see over the heads of people in front of us. People in authority stand to address a crowd. We stand for others to see us, as in church or a school assembly. We stand to give up our seat to someone in greater need of it; older people, who may find it hard to stand for long, accept gratefully.

In this series we will reflect on the times when Jesus stood up. These occasions tell us a lot about him and his ministry. May you discover more about him and experience Jesus, our risen Lord, who continually stands with us wherever we find ourselves.

The Bible passages in this section are the author's own abridged paraphrases, but based on and occasionally directly quoting the NIV.

Matthew 8:23–27

# Stood in a boat

**Jesus got into the boat with his disciples. Suddenly a furious storm broke over the lake. Waves swept over the boat. But Jesus was asleep. The disciples woke him, 'Lord, save us! We're going to drown!' Jesus replied, 'Why are you so afraid?' He stood up, rebuked the winds and waves, and it was completely calm... His disciples were amazed!**

I've walked in the hills when I was soaked to the skin and the wind made it almost impossible to remain upright. It would have been far more terrifying if I had been in a boat. Imagine just how petrified Jesus' disciples were. How long had they tried to save themselves before waking Jesus?

Jesus could remain asleep because he knew how storms, winds and waves worked. After all, he was present when the world came into being. He was, and is, the creator. When he woke and stood up, he was facing his created world, a world that had gone wrong ever since the fall. As Lord, as creator, he had the authority to command that calm order to be restored. His disciples hadn't yet grasped that. With Jesus, in their boat, there was no need to be afraid.

### ■ PRAYER

*Everything in our world comes under Jesus' rule. He's brought in the kingdom of God. Tell God what is causing you to fear right now. Ask him to calm that fear, as though you're in a boat and Jesus stands there with you.*

Luke 4:16–21

# Stood up to read

**One sabbath day in the synagogue, Jesus stood up to read from the prophet Isaiah: 'The Spirit of the Lord is on me, because he has anointed me to proclaim good news to the poor'… He rolled up the scroll and sat down. The eyes of everyone were fixed on him. Jesus announced, 'Today this scripture is fulfilled in your hearing.'**

I doubt any PE teacher sits at the start of a lesson and says, 'I know you don't like cross country running and today it's cold, but perhaps you could put on your kit.' Instead, the teacher stands to announce, 'It's cross country running today. You've five minutes to get your kit on.' It is all about having authority. The teacher expects children to accept what they're told to do.

Here Jesus stands up to read the sacred scriptures, God's word, to be read with authority and conviction. Imagine the authority with which Jesus read from the prophet Isaiah. He is reading about himself. The congregation is transfixed. They've never heard anything like it. Jesus explains, 'These ancient precious words are about me! Believe me. Take me seriously.'

### ■ PRAYER

*Every time we read the Bible, or hear the Bible read, we are opening ourselves to hear God's word for us. Pray that these words from Psalm 119 will be true for you: 'Open my eyes that I may see wonderful things in your law… your word is a lamp for my feet, a light on my path' (vv. 18, 105).*

Luke 18:35–43

# Stood still to heal

**A blind beggar sitting by the roadside as Jesus entered Jericho shouted out many times, 'Jesus, Son of David, have mercy on me!' Jesus stopped and stood still. 'What do you want me to do for you?' he asked the man. 'I want to see.' Jesus said, 'Your faith has healed you.' Immediately the man could see. He followed Jesus, praising God.**

At the Wimbledon tennis tournament, if you get a seat by the players' exit from the Centre Court, a top-ranked player, as they leave, might pause for five seconds to sign your programme. No more than six seconds. No eye contact.

That would not be long enough for this blind beggar. He has heard about Jesus' power to heal. He already believes Jesus can restore his sight. He is determined not to be ignored. It must have been obvious what the man wanted most of all. Jesus could have healed him in a matter of seconds. Instead, in this moment, as the man tells Jesus what he wants, Jesus stands to give the blind man 100% of his attention. Sight is restored. The man recognises this is God's work.

### ■ PRAYER

*God longs for us to tell him exactly what, deep in our hearts, we most desire for him to do. Even if you've already told him, tell him once again. Our desires are shaped the more we talk with God, and God is always ready to listen.*

John 7:37–39 (NIV)

# Stood up to proclaim

**On the last and greatest day of the festival, Jesus stood and said in a loud voice, 'Let anyone who is thirsty come to me and drink. Whoever believes in me, as Scripture has said, rivers of living water will flow from within them.' By this he meant the Spirit, whom those who believed in him were later to receive.**

The climax of any festival is usually the last day. Tickets for events on that day are harder to come by, though I doubt if people needed tickets for this seven-day annual Feast of Tabernacles in Jerusalem. The festival celebrated the recent harvest as well as God's provision for his people during their wanderings in the wilderness. Every day, water from the Pool of Siloam was poured out in the temple, offering special thanks for the rainfall necessary for a good harvest.

Jesus came into the temple to teach. On the last day, standing up, he made an impassioned speech, his voice echoing around. Influenced by the water at the festival, he offered to quench anyone's thirst for God. Once Jesus had returned to heaven, the Holy Spirit would come, bringing God's living water to bubble away forever inside those who believe in Jesus.

■ **PRAYER**

*As you take a sip of water, thank Jesus that his promise on this occasion is true for you too. Ask his Spirit to continue to become in you 'a spring of water welling up to eternal life' (John 4:14, NIV).*

John 19:5–11

# Stood for his trial

**Pilate, the Roman governor, said to the chief priests and their officials, 'Here is the man!' They shouted, 'Crucify! Crucify!' Later Pilate said to Jesus who stood before him, 'Don't you realise I have power to free you or crucify you?' Jesus answered, 'You would have no power over me if it were not given to you from above.'**

Judges in a courtroom sit on a raised platform, above everyone else present. Everyone stands when they enter. It's a statement of who is in charge. Jesus was accused by the Jewish and Roman authorities in his trial. Both subjected him to maximum humiliation. He was bound, mocked, slapped, dressed in a crown of thorns and a purple robe and physically flogged – all this even before his crucifixion. But his power remained undiminished. Still in control, he chose to be humiliated.

We're told Jesus stood before Pilate, who sat on a throne representing Roman authority. Jesus pointed out Pilate's claim to power was paper thin. The religious leaders stayed outside, not wanting to become 'unclean' by close association with non-Jews. Their power was limited to what the Romans granted them, though they tried to challenge Pilate's authority.

### ■ PRAYER

*Throughout this world, power is wielded unjustly, abusively and destructively. In God's sight this power is paper thin. Pray for one place in the world that troubles you, remembering that God 'will judge the world in righteousness and the peoples in his faithfulness' (Psalm 96:13, NIV).*

John 20:11–16

# Stands – resurrected

**Weeping, Mary looked inside the tomb and saw two angels sitting where Jesus' body had been. She said to them, 'Where have they put my Lord?' Turning around she saw Jesus standing there. She did not realise it was him. Thinking he was the gardener she asked him where he had put Jesus. Then Jesus said to her, 'Mary.'**

As a result of incomprehensible personal life events or world disasters, it's easy to become confused, reach the wrong conclusions, repeat ourselves or simply not cope. Jesus' disciples, including Mary Magdalene, were facing a tragic bereavement, betrayal by Judas Iscariot, disappointment that Jesus was not the Messiah they'd believed him to be and fear for their own lives.

How confusing for Mary to discover that the stone blocking the entrance to Jesus' tomb had been moved. She instinctively runs to tell the disciples, then comes back, desperately wanting to find Jesus' body. Seeing two angels inside the tomb, she blurts out, 'Where's Jesus gone?' and repeats the same question to the gardener. But this is no gardener. She can't understand how Jesus can be alive, but rejoices that he knows her name. There's time enough for making sense of that.

### ■ PRAYER

*However out of control life might seem, we can be reassured that Jesus knows us by name and comes to give us hope for the present and future. Begin praying to Jesus with these words, 'Jesus, you know me by name, inside out, so I want to tell you…'*

Luke 24:36–45

# Stands among them

**Jesus himself stood among them and said, 'Peace be with you.' The disciples were frightened, thinking they saw a ghost. He said, 'Look at my hands and my feet! Touch me and see; a ghost doesn't have flesh and bones.' Then he asked them, 'Do you have anything here to eat?' He opened their minds so they could understand the Scriptures.**

'I find it hard to believe,' we might say about something we'd describe as a miracle. New parents gaze in wonder at their newborn child. Is this real? A badly damaged relationship begins to heal. Is this possible? A friend with no time for God expresses an interest. Can it be true?

Jesus' disciples were stunned when the women claimed they'd encountered angels and Jesus. Apparently, he'd appeared to Simon and two people walking to Emmaus. Wishful thinking? A case of mistaken identity? Many try to explain away the reality of Jesus' resurrection.

Jesus was not a ghost. He backed this up by requesting food and offering an invitation to be touched. Still in shock, his disciples needed help to understand. We can't meet Jesus as they did since he's ascended to his Father. But by faith we know he's alive. His resurrection has destroyed the power of death.

■ **PRAYER**

*Just like the first disciples, we need our minds to be opened to grasp all that's said about Jesus in the scriptures. Ask him to continue by his Spirit to deepen your experience of the resurrected Jesus, alive within you.*

Acts 6:15; 7:51–56

# Stands to welcome

**Everyone looked at Stephen. His face seemed like an angel's. He continued, 'You stiff-necked people. Was there ever a prophet your ancestors did not persecute?' Hearing this, they dragged him out of the city to stone him. Stephen, full of the Holy Spirit, looking up to heaven, saw the glory of God and Jesus standing at the right hand of God.**

Throughout church history, Christians have been martyred for their faith. Stephen is known as the first. He was one of the key leaders of the church in Jerusalem, filled with the Spirit of God and blessed with gifts to perform great wonders and signs. These included the gift of preaching, judging by how he addressed the Sanhedrin (Jewish Council). He aroused strong opposition and was violently evicted from the building, to be stoned to death.

The ascended Jesus is usually described as sitting at his Father's right hand. But on this rare occasion, Stephen sees Jesus standing. Why standing? Maybe, since the Jewish leaders had rejected Stephen's call to accept Jesus as Messiah, Jesus stood to express his acceptance of Stephen's message. Maybe it reminded Stephen that Jesus himself stood before Pilate and the Jewish authorities. Maybe, put simply, Jesus stood to welcome Stephen. For whatever reason, this vision of the standing Jesus must have brought great comfort to Stephen.

### ■ PRAYER

*Ask Jesus to reassure you that he will welcome you into his presence to spend eternity with him, 'Good and faithful servant!'*

Acts 23:10–11

# Stands to encourage

**The Roman commander brought Paul before the Jewish Council, where a dispute over Paul's teaching became so violent the commander feared Paul would be torn to pieces. He ordered troops to bring Paul into the barracks. The following night the Lord stood near Paul and said, 'Take courage! You have testified about me in Jerusalem, so you must also testify in Rome.'**

Sometimes, we wake in the middle of the night and cannot get back to sleep. Our anxieties can get out of hand in the early hours. What do you do?

This story about Paul is less well-known. It's one I love and often return to. The apostle Paul has returned to Jerusalem. His Jewish opponents attempt to kill him and on two occasions nearly succeed. Paul is only saved by the intervention of Roman soldiers. The commander, knowing Paul was a Roman citizen, does not know what to do. Perhaps the Sanhedrin (Jewish Council) can enlighten him.

Imagine Paul's emotions at night, under guard in the barracks, fearing for his life. It's beautiful to read how the resurrected Jesus comes to stand near him, to reassure him. Jesus may not often speak to us like that, but he has promised never to forsake us.

■ **PRAYER**

*The psalmist boldly claims: 'God, you're my refuge. I trust in you and I'm safe!… Fear nothing – not wild wolves in the night… Not disease that prowls through the darkness' (Psalm 91:2, 5, MSG). Claim these words when you next toss and turn in your bed.*

Revelation 3:15, 19b–20 (NIV)

# Stands to knock

'I know your deeds, that you are neither cold nor hot. I wish you were either one or the other... So be earnest and repent. Here I am! I stand at the door and knock. If anyone hears my voice and opens the door, I will come in and eat with that person, and they with me.'

For several years I took a class of children to St Paul's Cathedral in London. Our tour included a viewing of Holman Hunt's famous, large painting, *Light of the World*. Jesus stands to knock on a door that is surrounded by weeds and thistles. This door has only one handle, on the other side. Jesus wears a crown and holds a lamp. The children were always curious.

John, who wrote the Revelation from Jesus Christ, was a prisoner on the island of Patmos. He heard, and then delivered, messages from Jesus to seven churches. His last message was to the church in Laodicea, a banking centre famous for its textiles and unique eye ointment. These Christians were no longer totally committed to Christ. John invites them to turn from their half-heartedness and recommit themselves, to open the door and welcome him in.

■ **PRAYER**

*This is a message for anyone whose joy in following Jesus has gone tepid, maybe for such reasons as distraction, disappointment or disillusionment. But Jesus still stands to welcome anyone who opens the door, even a chink. Pray for yourself, or for anyone you know whose faith in Christ has gone cold.*

# Jeremiah's journal

## Martyn Payne

**This word came to Jeremiah from the Lord: 'Take a scroll and write on it all the words I have spoken to you...' (Jeremiah 36:1–2, NIV)**

I wonder if you keep a diary or write reflections in a journal? I have diaries that go back to my primary school years (with a few gaps here and there!) and it's fascinating to occasionally dip back into these records of events from my early years. In rereading my later journal entries, I am always amazed at what God inspired me to write, as I recorded the highs and lows of my discipleship journey. It is one of the ways that God has spoken to me most powerfully.

In a similar way, the book of Jeremiah gives us glimpses into the prophet's experience of God, as he wrestled with the words God gave him to speak and the response to those words from God's people at the time. It's a journal that gives us insights into the grace of God, as well as encouragement as we read of Jeremiah's own honest outbursts of frustration and despair, alongside his heartfelt prayers of trust in God.

In the reflections that follow, I hope you will hear God's words as you face the inevitable ups and downs of being a disciple of Jesus. Jeremiah's circumstances may be very different from our own, but nevertheless, as people of faith, we can relate to his experience of God's presence, protection and peace, whatever life might throw at us.

Jeremiah 1:9 (NIV)

# Jeremiah's calling as God's prophet

**Then the Lord reached out his hand and touched my mouth and said to me, 'I have put my words in your mouth.'**

Jeremiah tells us he came from a priestly family and was called to be a prophet during the godly reign of King Josiah. He was overwhelmed to be chosen for this role while still a child, and he certainly did not feel worthy of the task before him. Yet the Lord reassured him of God's presence and inspiration, whatever might happen.

What a privilege to be God's spokesperson. As Christians filled with God's Spirit, this is a privilege we share with Jeremiah. God wants to speak life-giving and peaceable words through us to bless those we meet each day. In this part of his journal, Jeremiah records how God spoke to him through the almond tree near his home, and a pot boiling over. This reassured him, through a play on words, that God was watching over the judgement that was about to come on God's people.

Perhaps today, you need to remind yourself that God has chosen you; that God is watching over you and the words that you speak to others this day. I'm reminded of what was said of the prophet Samuel, namely that, 'none of [his] words fall to the ground' (1 Samuel 3:19).

### ■ PRAYER

*Lord, here are my lips, larynx and lungs – I offer them to you this day, to be your sound system, through which you might speak to a needy world. Amen*

Jeremiah 4:19 (NIV)

# Jeremiah's heartache as God's servant

'Oh, my anguish, my anguish! I writhe in pain. Oh, the agony of my heart! My heart pounds within me, I cannot keep silent.'

In this chapter of his journal, we hear not only the Lord's voice, but Jeremiah's too; and in particular, the cost to him of being God's chosen prophet. He's been given words to speak against his own people, and it breaks his heart to declare them. God had warned him that he would be saying tough things, but that didn't stop it being difficult.

Jeremiah is a very human prophet who struggles with the anguish that comes with his calling. He can see what judgement will mean for God's people and can imagine the devastation that lies ahead. He's neither detached, nor immune, from all that is happening and all that is to come.

There is much talk of the need for empathy and compassion today, and it's certainly something to aspire to in our relationships with those around us. If we are called to share God's words, we must also share God's heart. Jeremiah's experience reminds us that speaking for God goes hand in hand with feeling with God for those to whom we speak. It will mean weeping with those who weep and often sitting in silence alongside those who suffer.

■ **PRAYER**

*Open my heart, Lord, to the pain and anguish of others, and teach me how to speak for you by sometimes being the silent presence of your grace in time of need. Amen*

Jeremiah 9:23–24 (NIV)

# God's prayer-warrior

**This is what the Lord says: 'Let not the wise boast of their wisdom or the strong boast of their strength or the rich boast of their riches, but let the one who boasts boast about this: that they have the understanding to know me, that I am the Lord, who exercises kindness, justice and righteousness on earth, for in these I delight,' declares the Lord.**

This is an insightful entry in Jeremiah's journal about God's character, which is echoed by Paul in the New Testament where he writes: 'Let the one who boasts boast in the Lord' (1 Corinthians 1:31).

Jeremiah had a hard message to deliver, but in essence it boiled down to this: God's people should choose the way of humility. Yes, there had been idolatry, deceit and empty worship, but at the root of all this was pride. It is this arrogant attitude that Jeremiah weeps over; he is deeply wounded by what he saw in his day.

Are we similarly moved by arrogance in our times? Do we weep with God over the unjust and careless ways in which we treat our world and its people? All this pain and suffering breaks God's heart and of course was ultimately experienced by God's Son on the cross. Calvary is the awful focus point of God's lament for the world. Jeremiah comes close to Easter, even here in the depths of the Old Testament.

### ■ PRAYER

*Lord, when I listen to the news each day, help me not to be indifferent, but to share in your lament for justice and reconciliation. Turn my feelings into a heartfelt prayer that people will come to understand and know your love. Amen*

Jeremiah 14:9b (NIV)

# Jeremiah's prayers as God's child

**'You are among us, Lord, and we bear your name; do not forsake us!'**

Jeremiah writes this journal entry during a time of natural disaster. A drought has hit Judah, which should have prompted people to turn to the Lord; instead, they trust in the false prophecies of those who say 'all will be well'. That was the easy message to give and the comfortable one to hear; but it was a lie.

Despite their response, Jeremiah nevertheless engages in heartfelt prayer to God, even though they themselves have repeatedly rejected his message and even threatened his life. Remarkably Jeremiah does not give up on them, but intercedes on their behalf with two moving prayers (vv. 7, 19). He confesses Judah's sin and asks for forgiveness. These are the prayers of a remarkable man of God, who recognises that judgement is coming and yet he still cries for mercy. As we have already seen, he is a man of tears and prayer, and those two often go hand in hand.

Have you ever considered your calling to 'stand in the gap' and inter-cede for our world like this? Moses did it for the people of God in the wilderness at Mount Sinai; and of course, Jesus did it for us all when he prayed: 'Father, forgive them, for they do not know what they are doing' (Luke 23:34).

### ■ PRAYER

*'For the sake of your name, do not despise us… our hope is in you'*
*(vv. 21–22). Amen*

Jeremiah 17:7–8a (NIV)

# Jeremiah's psalm of faith

**'Blessed is the one who trusts in the Lord, whose confidence is in him. They will be like a tree planted by the water.'**

Throughout his long ministry, Jeremiah had little success. The people did not listen to him, but sadly chose their own downfall. Yet Jeremiah remained faithful to God.

In this journal entry, Jeremiah records a song, which is very like Psalm 1. In Jeremiah's version, however, the image of the tree comes second, and contrasts with the initial image of the tumbleweed, rolling rootless across the desert (vv. 5–6). It's a memorable description of those who decide to trust God, as opposed to those who don't.

Everything hinges on whether people are prepared to obey God's best for their lives. And by way of an example, he cites the fact that they are breaking God's commandment about the sabbath (vv. 19–27). The Jews were distinct in that they had no statue of their God and also did no work on one day every week. On both accounts, Jeremiah's generation had failed to display this distinctiveness. They hadn't listened to God. Jeremiah, however, lives a faithful life and this is his greatest witness.

I wonder what inspiration we can find here for ourselves, living out our Christian lives in an increasingly secular culture? How can we put down our roots and be a tree by the water, not a shrub blown by the wind?

### ■ PRAYER

*Sit with Jeremiah's words in verse 12: 'A glorious throne, exalted from the beginning, is the place of our sanctuary.'*

Jeremiah 18:6b (NIV)

# God speaks to Jeremiah through the everyday

**'Like clay in the hands of the potter, so are you in my hand, Israel.'**

Sometimes people ask us: 'How do you hear God speak?' There isn't one answer to this, but one way is illustrated in this entry in Jeremiah's journal. He is prompted to visit a pottery workshop, and while watching the potter throw, and then shape, a pot, he becomes aware of God's voice. The process often goes wrong, and the clay needs to be remoulded. In the same way, God is the Sovereign Potter who has a best plan for our lives, which he painstakingly pursues, despite our wilfulness as rebellious clay.

If we only open our eyes and ears, there are parables like this all around us. Jesus taught this way, using, for example, the seasons of sowing and harvest to teach about God's character. I wonder what similar everyday parables are around you today, as you listen out for God's voice?

Jeremiah passed on that everyday visual aid about God, and yet, as he records later in this chapter, the people refused to listen. Stubbornly they invite God to shape them for destruction, not mercy. No wonder in his next journal entry (chapter 19), Jeremiah takes a pot and smashes it in front of Jerusalem's elders as a sign of judgement.

### ■ PRAYER

*Holy Spirit, help me to hear God's voice this day and please also shape me into your best purposes for my life. Amen*

Jeremiah 27:4–5 (NIV, abridged)

# God's words through Jeremiah are uncomfortable

'This is what the Lord Almighty, the God of Israel, says: "… with my great power and outstretched arm I made the earth and its people and the animals that are on it, and I give it to anyone I please."'

Jeremiah made use of dramatic visual aids. Here he dresses up as a captive with a yoke across his shoulders, like a prisoner in a chain gang. And he chooses the occasion of a visiting delegation of kings to do this. Once he'd caught their attention, he passed on God's message.

To everyone's surprise, he told them that they should surrender to Nebuchadnezzar and not resist his armies. God is in charge of history, not them; this is the way it must be. Anyone who is offering another solution is a false prophet.

I wonder what this says to us today? Might we similarly be deceived into thinking that God's message is what we most want to hear? Are we willing to accept that doing something challenging and difficult might be the surprising way God is moving us? The truth was that Judah would have to lose everything before God could restore them. It was going to take the humiliation of exile before they learned to be God's people again. This is still the way for us too: the way of the cross.

■ **PRAYER**

*Open my ears, Lord, to hear what you're saying to me about my life and let me not be deceived into hearing only what I want to hear. Amen*

Jeremiah 29:7 (NIV)

# Jeremiah's ministry to those already in exile

**'Seek the peace and prosperity of the city to which I have carried you into exile. Pray to the Lord for it, because if it prospers, you too will prosper.'**

In this journal entry, we learn that Jeremiah's ministry was not just to Judah, but also to those already in exile. Some Jews had been taken into captivity and in that group were Daniel and Ezekiel. The Babylonians had exiled the cream of Judah's society, along with the city's wealth, and some of these people had been Jeremiah's friends.

So, the prophet writes them a letter, which contains great wisdom for all of us, who are, according to the book of Hebrews, 'foreigners and strangers on earth' (Hebrews 11:13) – disciples on our way home to heaven. Jeremiah is honest. There won't be a quick return – in fact, two generations will have to pass; so instead, they should pray for the people there and work for their good – their 'shalom'.

This is our calling too. We are here to bless and bring peace to our communities. As Jeremiah writes, God's promise is that: 'You will seek me and find me when you seek me with all your heart' (v. 13). God is not just in special places, but is everywhere. This is one of the great lessons that the people of God learned in exile.

### ■ PRAYER

*Reflect on the promise found in verse 11: '"I know the plans I have for you", declares the Lord, "plans… to give you hope and a future."'*

Jeremiah 33:3 (NIV)

# Jeremiah shares God's big picture for the future

**'Call to me and I will answer you and tell you great and unsearchable things you do not know.'**

We've reached the last years of King Zedekiah's reign, and Jerusalem is under siege. By now, Jeremiah's public ministry has been silenced and he's imprisoned in the royal guard house. His message of surrender would not be good for morale.

Nevertheless, he finds ways to speak. His message now is that God will bring them back from exile. They will experience forgiveness and restoration. And so, he buys a plot of land, even though it won't be possible to build on it for 70 years. Such is his faith in God's promises.

And he continues to keep his journal, including a remarkable prophecy that one day God will raise up a new righteous king and priest (33:16). Jeremiah is not just a prophet of doom, but one who has caught the big picture of God's love for the world, which was finally revealed in the life, death and resurrection of Jesus.

Jeremiah knew that God was on his side for the long term. It is this big vision that kept Jeremiah faithful; and his words are here to help us to trust in the one who will bring to completion the good work the Spirit has started in our lives.

■ **PRAYER**
*Thank you, Lord, that you are a God who loves to forgive and restore. Help us to be humble enough to keep returning to you each day, ready to start again. Amen*

Jeremiah 36:32 (NIV, abridged)

# Jeremiah's long-suffering and faithful ministry

**So Jeremiah took another scroll and gave it to the scribe Baruch... and as Jeremiah dictated, Baruch wrote on it all the words of the scroll that Jehoiakim king of Judah had burned in the fire.**

It's amazing that we still have Jeremiah's journal. The king was so angry when he heard its first edition read that he cut it into shreds and burnt it in the fire. Undeterred, Jeremiah started all over again.

Jeremiah's last days in Jerusalem are very dramatic. He ends up being thrown down a well and left to die, to become just another victim of the Babylonian siege. But God hears his cry from the depths and he is rescued by an Ethiopian servant of the king. Perhaps this outsider had heard Jeremiah preach, and believed him? In fact, God stays with Jeremiah to the very end, and his life is spared by King Nebuchadnezzar himself.

Jeremiah's prophecies all came true, and the last we hear of the prophet is of him being left behind in Jerusalem with the ones not taken to Babylon, and then escaping with some of them to Egypt.

Jeremiah's ministry may not have been successful, but it was faithful. As Jeremiah says to his friend, Baruch, near the end of his journal (45:5), don't seek great things for yourself. Living a life of humble trust in God is what constitutes true success, for each of us.

### ■ PRAYER

*Thank you, God, that Jesus said: 'I am with you always, to the very end of the age' (Matthew 28:20). Help me to trust in this life-changing promise for my life. Amen*

# The Gift of Years

 **Debbie Thrower** is the founder of BRF Ministries' Anna Chaplaincy for Older People. She retired in late 2023 and is now a vice president of BRF Ministries.

Visit **annachaplaincy.org.uk** to find out more.

**Debbie writes...**

Welcome!

TV's *The Repair Shop* shows just how attached we become to objects with sentimental value. A cherished Shove Ha'penny board my father passed down was a link to his own childhood, and now, for me and my children, evokes happy memories of high-spirited games at Christmas. Shove Ha'penny requires a super smooth shuffleboard, laid flat, and then you use your thumb or palm to scoot coins up the board. You gain points based on where they land. I'm pleased to see Derek Morgan focusing on the fun of such old-fashioned childhood games.

One recollection sparked by Derek's series was of my confirmation as a teenager, where my father got confirmed alongside me. We didn't have any deep and meaningful conversations about God and life at the time, but his step engendered a strong sense of solidarity.

As 2 Timothy says: 'I am reminded of your sincere faith, which first lived in your grandmother Lois and in your mother Eunice and, I am persuaded, now lives in you... from infancy you have known the Holy Scriptures' (1:5; 3:15, NIV). We give thanks for all the good influences on us, from our earliest days until now.

Best wishes

*Debbie*

# Grandparenting for Faith

**Becky Sedgwick's** *Grandparenting for Faith* was published in January 2024 and has become a best-seller for BRF Ministries, seeming to meet an important need. It's garnered huge praise from a wide range of commentators and reviewers, including this from Rachel Turner, founder of Parenting for Faith:

'This book is hopeful, realistic and deeply relevant to every grandparent, whether their grandchildren are babies, or adults with babies of their own.'

Becky shares the story behind the book:

One of the most exciting things I have learned about being a Christian is that if I am prepared to say 'Yes' to God, he has adventures for me. Some are small, others larger, but every time, no matter how crazy what he's suggesting seems, I discover that he will equip me to do it, and it will be fun!

God's agent in this case was Rachel Turner, founder of Parenting for Faith and author of multiple Parenting for Faith titles. In a team meeting about three years ago, she looked me in the eye and said, 'And Becky's going to write the Grandparenting for Faith book.' Me? But I'm not a grandparent and I've never written a book, I thought… but then I had an inkling that this was one of those God-adventures I knew I could trust.

Fast forward 18 months later and a book contract landed in my inbox. I was simultaneously excited and terrified, and taking a deep breath I plunged into the world of grandparenting.

I knew that the core content of Parenting for Faith – God's design for children and teens' discipleship and the five key tools for parents and carers to help their kids meet and know God – would be the same (find out more about the core content of Parenting for Faith at **parenting-forfaith.org**). What would be different would be how that worked for grandparents.

Very few are present daily in their grandchildren's lives; and there are the ever-present challenges of time, distance and family dynamics. Some grandparents are in the wonderful position of sharing their faith wholeheartedly with their children and grandchildren, but others may have to navigate different faiths or no faith, or be faced with hostility when they try to share their views.

I started by looking at the secular research on grandparenting, and it was fascinating. Turns out that grandparents are hugely influential just because they are grandparents, and that simply by having a grandparent present in their life, grandchildren are more stable and resilient. The research into the spiritual influence of grandparents was equally fascinating.

Grandparents are a very important part of children's faith journeys even when their parents don't have faith. We also decided to do our own research into how grandparents share their faith, and conducted a survey of Christian grandchildren, asking how their grandparents influenced their own faith.

And what a wonderful picture of grandparenting we gathered! In so many instances it was stories of ordinary everyday grandparents loving well and just being themselves with God – and having an impact far beyond what they ever could have imagined.

In fact, when we interviewed Christian grandparents about how they shared their faith with their grandchildren, most of them really didn't think they were doing anything in particular – but it turns out it's the ordinary everyday lived faith which grandchildren spot, consider and see.

I hope that this book will serve as a handbook for Christian grandparents, which they can look through, mark up and return to as their grandparenting – and their grandchildren – change. My prayer is that it helps grandparents see that they are part of God's plan for their grandchildren's discipleship and to give them tools, ideas and confidence to share all who God is for them with the children they love the most.

To find out more about *Grandparenting for Faith* go to **brfonline.org.uk/grandparenting-for-faith**.

**Grandparenting for Faith**
*Sharing God with the children you love the most*
Becky Sedgwick
978 1 80039 204 5
**brfonline.org.uk**

# Alone in the hills

 **Glynda Winterson** is one of our favourite poets and she has recently published a new collection called *Sweeping the Sea*. One reviewer has commented: 'These are delicate, tender poems that say a resounding "yes" to life, negotiating with honesty and grace the strange miracle of existence and the potential for faith in the face of certain pain and loss.'

Some of her poems are more overtly Christian than others, but they are all imbued with a spirit that is, in the words of another reviewer, 'fierce, elemental… and ultimately redemptive'.

We are grateful to Glynda for permission to publish this poem from her new collection. She says of the poem:

'It inspires worship and love and gives me great comfort and encouragement to know that Jesus the Son of God experienced what it is like to be human. When we pray we can be sure that Christ understands our feelings and emotions, including loneliness and the need to be fully known and understood, as in this poem.

'Yet it is still a mystery where this poem came from! "Alone in the hills", like all my poems, was begun without me knowing what it would be about or how it would end! A single phrase came to mind and I recognised it would grow to become a poem! And it did!'

## Alone in the hills

*From the full moon*
*enough reflected light*
*to make a shadow of himself.*

*He is here to pray.*
*He has become a man*
*of prayer and now*

*alone in the hills,*
*far from home, needing*
*in this moment*
*to be known and understood*

*there is comfort in his father's*
*all-encompassing view*

*of the north and south*
*the east and west beyond*
*one tiny country's inland sea*

*storm-blown below him now*

*where his disciples*
*struggling to believe*

*are rowing through the night*
*against the contradiction of the four winds.*

By Glynda Winterson, used with kind permission.

Copies of Glynda's new collection, *Sweeping the Sea,* can be bought from the poet for £7.00 including postage. Please contact **enquiries@ brf.org.uk** or call 01865 319700 and your request will be passed on.

# Death and life: A church's guide to exploring mortality

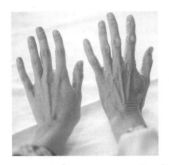

In the spring of 2024 BRF Ministries published *Death & Life: A church's guide to exploring mortality*: a rich, research-based resource for churches to help people reflect on death and mortality as part of the process of healthy aging. As a society we're not good at talking about death but there's strong evidence to show that people of all ages welcome opportunities to do so.

Lead author Joanna Collicutt writes: 'Reflecting on our own death can enable us to live more fully in the here and now because the issues that come into sharp focus as death approaches turn out to be the same issues that are important in living life well.' The writers have identified six themes that encapsulate these important issues: loving, letting go, seeing, growing, belonging and hoping. This moving meditation by Robert Glenny is taken from the section on 'Loving'.

## Hands

You can tell a lot about someone by how their hands look. Size or skin complexion give clues as to a person's age. Callouses or marks may point to types of employment that require working with one's hands, and tanning may indicate whether that takes place inside or outside. A wedding ring will tell you a person's marital status, as will the faded line of the place where a ring once rested. Nails, bitten or chewed might tell you that this person's hands belong to an agitated body; perfectly manicured cuticles might tell you that this person takes pleasure in the way their hands are seen and enjoyed.

And hands can also convey a vast range of human behaviours and emotions. They can be stretched out in embrace; lifted up in surrender; held gently in a moment of intimacy. Hands can point, or stroke, or wave. They can greet with the raised palm of a high-five, the powerful grasp of a handshake, or the naked aggression of a fist.

They pervade our language. Those who are a dab hand at a task may gain the upper hand on those who aren't. We lend a helping hand to those in trouble; we ask for a hand in marriage; we give a big hand to those we approve of; we avoid falling into the wrong hands. If we live hand to mouth, then we would do well not to bite the hand that feeds us. If we are unable to do anything, it may be that our hands are tied. Something imminent may be close at hand; on the other hand it may be far away.

Isaiah 49:16 talks of God's hands: God says to Israel: 'See, I have inscribed you on the palms of my hands.' Earlier in the chapter, we read 'the Lord called me before I was born' (v. 1). You were known, before you were capable of knowledge. There was no time when God's love for you was not etched into his very being. God knows you like the back of his hand.

These are hands of boundless creativity, epic scale, vast beauty and unimaginable breadth. As Graham Kendrick wrote, they are 'hands that flung stars into space'. Yet upon this everlasting canvas we find our name inscribed, and we see that tiny as we are, we are known intimately, completely and eternally. There is no time when God has known us and not loved us, or loved us and not known us.

A few days before he died, Jesus gathered with his disciples. He knows that the hour for his own departure from this world is near. He also knows that shortly he will be betrayed by Judas into the hands of the authorities, by Peter who will refuse to be recognised as his companion and by the rest who will scatter and flee.

As the burden of this knowledge weighs heavy upon Jesus, still in this moment he loves them and loves them to the end. In this moment of extreme turmoil, knowledge and love meet in the most intimate of encounters. Jesus washes the feet of every disciple, removes his outer garments, emptying himself in the form of a servant to leave a legacy of love. Judas departs from their presence and Jesus tells those who remain that this is how they are to be known to others: as those who love, just as they have been loved.

When we come close to our own death we want to tell those close to us that we know them and that we love them, and we want to hear that we have been known and loved. When life ends, knowledge and love are brought together in us as they always have been in God. We can say that to our beloved with a gentle squeeze of our hands. Then we place our hands in God's and know that love makes us inseparable from them.

To find out more about *Death & Life: A church's guide to exploring mortality* (£24.99) and the set of reflection cards (£8.99) created to accompany the course please go to **brfonline.org.uk/death-life**.

# In hope and trust

## Lin Ball

Looking back to your younger days, do you remember how it felt to stand on the brink of possibilities? What career would you choose? What ambitions would direct you? Hopefully you experienced some sense of expanding horizons as you moved into adulthood.

Advancing years sometimes feel like quite the reverse... a series of contractions. Those restrictions might be health challenges or reduced means. Whatever they are, how can we ensure that these aspects of our circumstances don't shrink the quality of our lives, in particular, our spiritual lives?

Can we still adventure with God?

I believe that within the warm encompassing of God's love we can still have experiences that are rich and fulfilling. Within the fold of his community, relationships can continue to grow and deepen. The human mind and heart are endlessly flexible and can be guided by his possibilities, not our limitations.

Our reflections will range Bible-wide, seeking inspiration to hope and trust in times of challenging transition. In the word of God we can find encouragement for leaning closer into God himself, and for finding strength and hope in belonging to the people of God.

**2 Corinthians 4:16–17 (AMP)**

# Renewed daily

**Therefore we do not become discouraged [spiritless, disappointed, or afraid]. Though our outer self is [progressively] wasting away, yet our inner *self* is being [progressively] renewed day by day. For our momentary, light distress [this passing trouble] is producing for us an eternal weight of glory [a fullness] beyond all measure [surpassing all comparisons, a transcendent splendour and an endless blessedness]!**

Like many Bible verses, this is both a wonderful encouragement and a massive challenge. The truth is that I am often tempted to be 'spiritless, disappointed, or afraid' as the years vanish. I had imagined that advancing years would bring certainty, yet the big questions of life have never seemed less black and white.

But there are many things of which I have never been more sure. Like my confidence in the eternal life to come. Does this mean that my grip on this world is weakening? Its attractions certainly appeal less. If my thoughts linger more on the life to come, does that signify the inner self being renewed?

Whatever the answers to those questions, we can embrace the difficult transitions of life more wholeheartedly when we remember the renewal that the Holy Spirit is always working within us.

### ■ PRAYER

*'Breathe on me, Breath of God, fill me with life anew, that I may love the way you love, and do what you would do' (Edwin Hatch, 1835–1889). Ask God to make this real to you, especially if you are feeling dispirited today.*

Psalm 46:1–3, 7 (NIV)

# Roaring and quaking

**God is our refuge and strength, an ever-present help in trouble. Therefore we will not fear, though the earth give way and the mountains fall into the heart of the sea, though its waters roar and foam and the mountains quake with their surging… The Lord Almighty is with us; the God of Jacob is our fortress.**

Praise God for the 'quiet waters' periods of our lives. But inevitably they are punctuated by turbulent times. The unexpected diagnosis, the death of a loved one, the betrayal, the bad news coming completely out of the blue. Such life events can shake us to the core – just like an earthquake, emotionally and sometimes physically.

A sense of perspective can help. I stand back and remind myself that I'm only one of millions down the years who have faced such setbacks. The human condition is essentially one of change and challenge; and we don't have to look far to find others who are also facing big issues.

More importantly, remaining resilient in shifting seasons is a gift to all those who trust in a constant and all-powerful companion: 'the God of Jacob is our fortress'. When the sand gives way beneath our feet, it's good to reach out to his unchanging strength.

### ■ PRAYER

*Ask God for the gift of resilience. In the words of St Teresa of Ávila: 'Let nothing disturb you, let nothing frighten you, all things are passing away; God never changes. Patience obtains all things. Whoever has God lacks nothing; God alone suffices.' Amen*

Romans 12:5–6a (AMP)

# Be a builder

**So we, who are many, are [nevertheless just] one body in Christ, and individually [we are] parts one of another [mutually dependent on each other]. Since we have gifts that differ according to the grace given to us, *each of us is to use them accordingly*.**

As I write this, I've been widowed just over 18 months, and hard on the heels of the grief is a desperate aloneness I've never experienced before. Married at 20 – which wasn't so usual in 1971 – I've never lived on my own, until now. When I can't sleep at 2.00 am I feel I could be the only person in the world.

Yet friendship and community have never been so vital to me, and I know it's where I have to invest in future days. Particularly, I must feel I belong to the 'one body in Christ' Paul talks about here. I need to experience that mutual interdependence, to know I have a role in sharing the gifts I have and to be on the receiving end of the gifts of others. I need to be a community builder, to give to others so that they can bless me. I need to belong.

### ■ PRAYER

*Give me the grace, Father God, to give myself away generously rather than hold on to what I have and so make myself poorer. Help me to advance rather than retreat, to grow in belonging rather than fade into aloneness. Make me a kingdom builder. Amen*

Ecclesiastes 3:1, 11 (NKJV)

# New season

**To everything there _is_ a season, a time for every purpose under heaven... He has made everything beautiful in its time. Also He has put eternity in their hearts, except that no one can find out the work that God does from beginning to end.**

Trying to second-guess God is time wasted. Frequently, when we think we have the way ahead planned, a spanner is thrown into the works, the wheels come off the trolley, diversion signs block the road.

But while the future remains a mystery, I believe that what God teaches us in the current season of life often prepares us for the next. Trusting in him limits any shock we might feel at the twists and turns, the unexpected outcomes. So when change comes we can dig deep into the treasury of what God has shown us along the way and we will hopefully find there's a current application. He does not leave us unprepared.

While I was writing this series I tripped pretty dramatically in the garden and fell headlong, fracturing my kneecap in several places as I impacted the paving slabs. In a split second my plans for the coming months were completely overturned. Plan B! Except that God knew all along. So what does he have to teach me in this?

■ **PRAYER**

_Father, I don't always understand your purposes. Help me renew my trust in your plan. Holy Spirit, invade my heart today and 'make beautiful' this time in my life. Amen_

Psalm 119:105, 107, 111 (MSG abridged)

# Check the map!

**By your words I can see where I'm going; they throw a beam of light on my dark path... Everything's falling apart on me, God; put me together again with your Word... I inherited your book on living; it's mine forever – what a gift! And how happy it makes me!**

You know what they say (stereotypically!) about men not wanting to consult maps? I lost count of the number of times I shouted at my husband in frustration: 'Would you please pull over so we can look at the route!'

But I find the Holy Spirit whispering (not shouting!) the same thing to me these days. It often takes me far too long to realise I've lost my way and need to pull over and check the map.

Perhaps it's one of the failings of getting older... to assume we know exactly how to get from A to B without thinking. The thing is, even if we're familiar with the roads, perhaps God wants us to take another route this time around?

The word of God is our manual for transition, our guide for the way forward, and we can so easily get lost without it.

■ **PRAYER**

*Thank you so much, Father God, for giving us your 'book on living'. Help me to seek out its directions today and at all the turning points in my life. Amen*

Isaiah 43:18–19 (GNT)

# Looking ahead

**The Lord says, 'Do not cling to events of the past or dwell on what happened long ago. Watch for the new thing I am going to do. It is happening already – you can see it now! I will make a road through the wilderness and give you streams of water there.'**

One of my greatest fears in getting older is living too much in the past! I see it often as I chat with friends. Our conversations can be a giveaway. We talk about 'the good old days.' We make unfavourable comparisons between today and 'the way things used to be.' We revisit and repeat familiar anecdotes. We relate things that God did for us many years ago.

While it's always good to remember God's past goodness, our eyes also need to be focused on the here and now, and on the ahead. What's God going to do in my life today? How will he use me tomorrow? To keep on growing we need to be willing to let go of the old and welcome the new, even when what's ahead is unknown or even unwelcome.

### ■ PRAYER

*Affirm your trust in God for the future with this beautiful prayer of Columba (c. 521–97): 'Alone with none but you, my God, I journey on my way. What need I fear when you are near, O King of night and day? More safe am I within your hand, than if a host did round me stand.'*

1 Timothy 6:6–8, 10a (KJV)

# Contentment

**But godliness with contentment is great gain. For we brought nothing into this world, and it is certain we can carry nothing out. And having food and raiment let us be therewith content... For the love of money is the root of all evil.**

My needs are more modest as I get older, and I think that's generally true of my friends. Some of the clothes in my wardrobe are well over 20 years old and I pride myself on keeping them neat. Mindful of the climate emergency, I travel infrequently. I recycle. I repurpose things. I simply buy less.

And thank goodness... because my income is static and doesn't stretch as far. The post-pandemic cost of living volatility has affected how secure I feel financially, even while I am aware that God has blessed me materially and others are struggling more. But financial vulnerability is an opportunity to grow in trusting God. This is another potential fear trap that I can surrender to him.

Contentment is an undervalued virtue. It's surely a better ambition for life than happiness. Happiness is disrupted as soon as something difficult happens, while contentment is prepared and embraces it.

■ **PRAYER**

*Settle my fears, Father God. Align my ambitions to your will. May I learn contentment from your Son, who set aside his heavenly kingdoms and power to live on earth in humility. Amen*

Psalm 103:2–5 (KJV)

# Light a candle

**Bless the Lord, O my soul, and forget not all his benefits: who forgiveth all thine iniquities; who healeth all thy diseases; who redeemeth thy life from destruction; who crowneth thee with lovingkindness and tender mercies; who satisfieth thy mouth with good things; so that thy youth is renewed like the eagle's.**

Though far from being a philosopher, my mum liked her little truisms and one was this: 'Old age doesn't come alone.' It was shorthand for the many things about ageing she could have done without. Few of us arrive in later life without being encumbered en-route with health problems, family distress, financial anxieties or other significant challenges.

I love the Celtic saying: 'It is better to light a candle than to curse the darkness.' An attitude of gratitude is a huge asset as we face difficult transitions. Accentuating the positive will give us resilience on the greyest of days. This is not denial of reality. It's not being a 'Pollyanna'. It's focusing on 'all his benefits' the psalmist rejoices in. He says that remembering the good things about a life of faith is like a renewal of youthfulness. Maybe that's because an aspect of youth is optimism.

### ■ PRAYER

*Light a candle in your heart for all the 'benefits' of your life today. Thank God for your salvation, for all the times he's answered your prayers, for his beautiful creation, for those you love and for those who love you. What else makes you grateful to him?*

Revelation 21:5–7 (CEV, abridged)

# True and to be trusted

**Then the one sitting on the throne said: I am making everything new… My words are true and can be trusted. Everything is finished! I am Alpha and Omega, the beginning and the end. I will freely give water from the life-giving fountain to everyone who is thirsty. All who win the victory will be given these blessings.**

My body lets me down more than it used to. My energy fails miserably at times. I know if I rely on my own resources then my prospects for adventure are limited, so I want to choose to trust in the God who opens up the horizon ahead and beckons me on.

Do you know that team building exercise beloved of corporates: the trust fall? Someone stands in the middle of the circle of their co-workers, closes their eyes and falls in any direction, trusting that they will be caught and held.

I imagine God and his angels encircling me sometimes when I'm facing a difficult decision or event. 'Go on! Trust me! I'll be there to catch you! I promise!'

■ **PRAYER**

*Your words, Father God, are true and to be trusted. Thank you for calling me to the great adventure of having faith in you. I want every day to count! 'Take myself, and I will be ever, only, all for thee' (Francis R. Havergal, 1836–79). Amen*

Daniel 2:20–22 (NIV)

# In his control

'Praise be to the name of God forever and ever; wisdom and power are his. He changes times and seasons; he deposes kings and raises up others. He gives wisdom to the wise and knowledge to the discerning. He reveals deep and hidden things; he knows what lies in darkness, and light dwells with him.'

What dreams did you have when you were younger? Take a moment to reflect on them. I dreamt of being a writer and having children – and God helped me make that a reality. But some dreams have died a death. I know I'll never have that little bookshop on the south coast now! And that's alright.

Thomas Merton (1915–68), an American monk, poet and writer, said this: 'You do not need to know precisely what is happening, or exactly where it is all going. What you need is to recognise the possibilities and challenges offered by the present moment, and to embrace them with courage, faith and hope' (*Conjectures of a Guilty Bystander*, Doubleday, 1966, p. 188). Today we might call that 'living mindfully', or 'being present'. That, together with an understanding that ultimately our powerful God is sovereign over all, is a recipe for inner peace.

■ **PRAYER**

*Father, I can say with the Psalmist, 'My times are in your hands' (Psalm 31:15). Thank you for all the joy you have given me. Even as I lay all my unrealised ambitions at your feet, give me that deep peace that comes from a surrendered life. Amen*

# Fun and games

## Derek Morgan

Many years ago, when you and I were considerably younger than we are today and before the invention of computer games and hand-held games consoles, we would amuse ourselves with a whole variety of indoor games, a veritable compendium in fact.

So many of those games were very simple and yet they would provide hours of entertainment for us, and I can imagine our parents sighing with weariness as we demanded to play our favourite game again and again and again. Games such as Happy Families or Snap would be played with family and friends seated round a table or, more likely, sitting on the carpet in front of the fire. I'm not sure I would want to get down there and play on the floor today.

I've recently come to realise that with a little bit of insight – or is it spiritual imagination – those simple children's games can actually reveal important life principles. Over the next ten reflections I will use games you may know well to show the wonderful truths they can teach us today.

Please enjoy them and be blessed.

Psalm 23:4 (NLT)

# Snakes and ladders

**Even when I walk through the darkest valley, I will not be afraid, for you are close beside me. Your rod and your staff protect and comfort me.**

I'm sure everyone must have played snakes and ladders when they were small. Oh, the joy of landing on the bottom of a ladder and zooming up that board. Sadly, there was the frustration and maybe a tantrum or two when you landed on the head of a long, long snake. Interestingly, when the game was played in India (where it originated) the board had many more snakes than ladders, but when it was introduced to the UK in the 1890s the Victorian folk thought it was fairer to have the same number of each.

As you look back through life, you may remember those periods when everything was going well for you and it seemed you could do no wrong. Equally, you may be saddened to remember those other periods when everything was going wrong. Have you ever wondered where God was at those times? Did you think he was close to you in the 'ladder' periods and he had abandoned you during those 'snake' periods? You may feel he is not there, but actually, he is only a prayer away. Jesus promises 'Be sure of this: I am with you always, even to the end of the age' (Matthew 28:20).

■ **PRAYER**

*Thank you, Lord, that you are always with me and will never forget me. Amen*

Jeremiah 29:11 (NIV)

# Jigsaw puzzle

'For I know the plans I have for you,' declares the Lord, 'plans to prosper you and not to harm you, plans to give you hope and a future.'

Which of us hasn't done a jigsaw at some time or other? Maybe as a young child you had a puzzle with about 12 chunky wooden pieces, but now you can skilfully complete that 1,000-piece monster. You know only too well that frustration of holding a piece in your hand and not being able to find where it fits. Now, imagine doing that jigsaw if you didn't have the picture on the box to look at. You'd have no idea where anything fits.

Have you ever seen life like that, where you are that odd piece? You wander through life never feeling you quite fit in. Sometimes, you think you may have found the right place, but soon you feel like you are being squashed into a hole that isn't quite the same shape that you are.

We can make our own decisions, but if we don't seek God's will, they may not be the best for us. God holds our jigsaw picture in his hands all the time and he knows exactly where we fit perfectly.

■ **PRAYER**

*Thank you, Father, that you know what is best for me. Help me never to forget to seek your guidance through the puzzle of life. Amen*

Luke 12:15 (NIV)

# Beat your neighbours

'Watch out! Be on your guard against all kinds of greed; life does not consist in an abundance of possessions.'

Beat your neighbours is a card game my brother and I used to love playing as children, and I can remember its box became very worn out and tatty. The idea was to gain more cards than everyone else and thereby become the winner. It was particularly intriguing because you could get to the point where one player was almost out of cards but, just by the luck of the draw, they could slowly gain more and more cards and eventually become the winner. Apparently, the mathematicians say the game has the potential to be never ending.

Something else that can be never-ending is the one-upmanship and jealousy that can exist between neighbours or even friends. Wanting a better car, a nicer handbag or a more exotic holiday are all examples of things that can be sought after. While the world may tempt us this way, Jesus would say that we should be sharing things with our neighbour, particularly if we have been blessed with plenty ourselves. Conversely, if you don't have all the nice things your neighbour has, don't be jealous of them. Or to put it another way, 'Do not desire another man's... cattle, his donkeys, or anything else that he owns' (Exodus 20:17, GNT). What would you do with their oxen anyway?

■ **PRAYER**

*Heavenly Father, help us to share what we have with others because we know that all things come from you. Amen*

Matthew 13:45–46 (NIV)

# Marbles

**'The kingdom of heaven is like a merchant looking for fine pearls. When he found one of great value, he went away and sold everything he had and bought it.'**

I'm sure you must have looked at a marble and wondered how they get those colourful swirly bits inside the glass ball. Marbles have that lovely combination of being pretty to look at and very tactile in the hand. When I was a young boy, though, games of marbles in the school playground were cut-throat. The aim was always to win the other boys' marbles without losing too many of your own – especially your favourite one!

But then there are other marbles – even more special than your favourite – that are not designed to be flicked across the floor but to demonstrate the glass blower's artistry and skill. Antique marbles from the 1800s are highly sought after by collectors and can be quite valuable: a single rare marble could cost you £20,000 at auction.

In the Bible passage above, the merchant gave everything he had to acquire that precious 'pearl'. Have you ever realised that this passage also applies to you? You are so precious to God that he gave everything… he gave Jesus up to die as the price to be paid to save you for eternity. However you may be feeling about yourself today, God says, 'You were worth it!'

### ■ PRAYER

*Thank you, Lord Jesus, that you went to the cross to save me. May I never forget your sacrifice for me. Amen*

John 14:6 (NIV)

# Puzzle maze

**Jesus answered, 'I am the way and the truth and the life. No one comes to the Father except through me.'**

When you were a child you likely had a puzzle book containing dot-to-dots, word-searches and mazes. I remember enjoying puzzle mazes where, for example, you would have three cartoon fishermen on one side and one cartoon fish on the other, and between them was a square maze with paths going all ways and only one reached the end. You had to start drawing a line around the maze from each fisherman to see who it was that caught the fish. As you grew older you no doubt worked out that the easiest way to find the answer was to start at the end and work back the other way.

In many respects, that maze is a bit like the journey of our spiritual life, where the final destination is heaven. People try different routes that they think will get them there. Things such as 'good works', 'being a nice person' or 'following a particular religion'. Fortunately, the God of heaven gave us the answer and, just like with the puzzle maze, we can work back from there. The Bible tells us which path to take and that is through faith in Jesus. All other paths are dead ends.

### ■ PRAYER

*Thank you, that if we confess that Jesus is Lord and believe in our heart that God raised him from the dead, we will be saved! Amen*

Hebrews 10:25 (NLT)

# Happy families

'Let us not neglect our meeting together, as some people do, but encourage one another, especially now that the day of his return is drawing near.'

Do you remember Mr Soot the sweep, Mrs Bun the baker's wife, Master Bones the butcher's son, or what about Miss Pots the painter's daughter? Happy Families is a game that can begin very quietly as you start to collect a set of cards in a certain family and then, just as you have one more card to go for the set, somebody else takes all three of your cards and they get the family. So frustrating!

That idea of families being father, mother and two children seems very outdated today when families come in so many different shapes and sizes. Whatever the shape of your family, sadly, it may have changed again in more recent years. You may find yourself living on your own because your loved one has now died, or maybe your children live a long distance away and rarely visit. Life can become very lonely if we don't have a family around us. But the family of God is never far away. If you are not in touch with a church or if you go to one but don't really speak to anybody, I encourage you to get involved, be open to making new friends and to feel the love and support of a church family around you.

■ **PRAYER**
*Thank you, Lord, for the family of God. May those who are lonely find a loving church family, and may those already in the family always give a warm welcome. Amen*

## John 8:12 (NLT, abridged)

# Snap!

**Jesus… said, 'I am the light of the world. If you follow me, you won't have to walk in darkness, because you will have the light that leads to life.'**

One of the easiest card games for children to play has to be Snap. The game tends to speed up as the players rush to put their card down and hope to get that all important match. It can become exceedingly rowdy too, with a noise like a bunch of angry snakes as the players start saying 'Sssssss' in readiness to shout 'Snap!' at the appropriate time. To be triumphant in the game, you just need to follow the person before you and do the exact same thing they did.

That got me to thinking… Jesus said something very similar. He would often say 'Follow me' to the people he met and he regularly had crowds of people following him. If we want to be triumphant in our daily living, we should follow him too. We can't follow him physically of course, but we can follow his ways and try to do the same sort of things that he did when he lived on earth. In order to do that, we need to know the Bible, learn his ways from our Christian friends and then follow his ways ourselves.

### ■ PRAYER

*Lord Jesus, we want to be your followers and walk in the light. Help us to learn from your Holy Spirit and to stay in tune with you. Amen*

Matthew 7:12 (NLT)

# Pass the parcel

**'Do to others whatever you would like them to do to you. This is the essence of all that is taught in the law and the prophets.'**

Now here's a game that has a real mix of excitement, suspense, disappointment and elation. I'm sure you remember sitting in a circle while that big bundle of delights was passed around, anxiously hoping the music would stop while you had it. That disappointment when it passed you by and the joy when it didn't, and you were able to unwrap one layer and maybe get a sweet or a small toy. I remember some children trying to hang on to the parcel rather than passing it on and their mums shouting at them to comply.

Sometimes in life we can see other people being blessed in some way and feel disappointment that it wasn't us. Other times, we might be the ones who receive a blessing and we can then celebrate and be joyful. The question is, when you receive a blessing, are you like that child who wants to hang on to it or do you pass it on and bless others because God has blessed you? John the Baptist said: 'If you have two shirts, give one to the poor. If you have food, share it with those who are hungry' (Luke 3:11).

### ■ PRAYER

*Heavenly Father, help us to treat others as we would wish to be treated and to bless them when we can. Amen*

Psalm 127:1 (NIV)

# Chess

**Unless the Lord builds the house, the builders labour in vain. Unless the Lord watches over the city, the guards stand watch in vain.**

I think chess is one of those games you either take to and really enjoy playing or you decide very early on that it really isn't the game for you. I probably put myself in the former category, though I haven't played for a long time.

Chess is all about forward planning, trying to anticipate what dangers you might face and having an answer to them. Too often, however, you just don't realise the danger you are in until you hear those fateful words 'Check-mate'. I dare say you would agree that life can be very much like that. How many times have you made plans to do something or go somewhere, then circumstances suddenly change and totally mess things up.

The Bible tells us that we need to seek God before making important decisions in life. We may plan to do this or do that and then maybe as an afterthought ask God to bless our plans, but that's rather the wrong way round. We should seek God first. As it says in Proverbs 16:3 'Put God in charge of your work, then what you've planned will take place' (MSG).

## ■ PRAYER

*Heavenly Father, forgive us for the times we go our own way and don't turn to you for your direction. Amen*

Revelation 3:20 (NLT)

# Dominoes

'Look! I stand at the door and knock. If you hear my voice and open the door, I will come in, and we will share a meal together as friends.'

Dominoes are great fun for those who don't even know how to play Dominoes. Who can resist standing all the dominoes on their ends in a long snake-like line, then knocking the first one over and watching as they tumble one after another. Great fun!

When I was thinking about these games from my childhood, I realised the behaviour of that line of dominoes was a great analogy for my own spiritual situation at a certain stage in my life. I had lined up excuse after excuse as to why I didn't believe the claims of Jesus and why I didn't want to live my life according to some dusty old book.

I only went to church because my girlfriend did, but one Sunday the sermon was based on the passage in the Bible where Jesus says he is knocking at my door and he wants to come in. In an instant, it was as if Jesus tapped on that first domino. All my excuses and obstructions just tumbled down and I said 'Yes!' to Jesus. That decision was a long time ago now and I haven't regretted it for one moment. I wonder, do you still have a line of dominoes between you and Jesus?

### ■ PRAYER

*Lord Jesus, thank you that once we say 'Yes' to you, you give us a life of joy and peace because of your eternal love for us. Amen*

# God is in control

*Then Job answered the Lord: 'I know that you can do all things and that no purpose of yours can be thwarted.'*

**JOB 42:1-2 (NRSV)**

We sometimes forget the more cheerful ending of the book of Job. As we have continued to live through challenging times, be that on personal, national and international levels, the reminder that God has it all under control is a reassuring promise to hold on to.

In this season, the Living Faith team are providing materials for Lent and Easter, and our collection of Easter and everyday cards is growing. Meanwhile, resources for Advent and Christmas are being prepared.

The Anna Chaplaincy, Messy Church and Parenting for Faith teams continue to offer training, resources and events supporting individuals and churches with their invaluable work, which really does enable people to grow in Christian faith across all ages and to know God cannot be thwarted.

We believe this work is invaluable, and we are assured of this by the kind feedback we receive. However, none of this would be possible without kind donations from individuals, churches charitable trusts and gifts in wills. If you would like to support us now and in the future you can become a Friend of BRF Ministries by making a monthly gift of £2 a month or more – we thank you for your friendship.

Find out more at **brf.org.uk/donate** or get in touch with us on on **01235 462305** or via **giving@brf.org.uk**.

We thank you for your support and your prayers.

*The fundraising team at BRF Ministries*

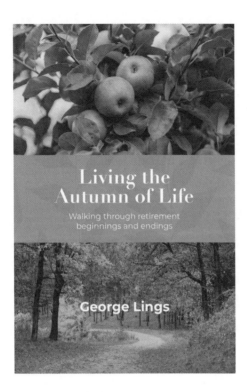

Autumn is a time of gains and losses: fruit being harvested, and leaves falling. This book charts the experience of living through both realities, drawn from the author's own life and from the views of interviewees. Informed by historical and contemporary reading, it offers snapshots of later life, taken against a backdrop of ageism in society and church. George Lings reflects on the identity of the 'active elderly', and considers through a biblical lens the challenges and opportunities that this season brings.

**Living the Autumn of Life**
*Walking through retirement beginnings and endings*
George Lings
978 1 80039 281 6  £12.99
**brfonline.org.uk**

# To order

Online: **brfonline.org.uk**
Telephone: +44 (0)1865 319700
Mon–Fri 9.30–17.00
Post: complete this form and send to the address below

Delivery times within the UK are
normally 15 working days. Prices are
correct at the time of going to press
but may change without prior notice.

| Title | Issue | Price | Qty | Total |
|---|---|---|---|---|
| Living the Autumn of Life | | £12.99 | | |
| Bible Reflections for Older People (single copy) | Jan–Apr 2025 | £5.55 | | |
| Bible Reflections for Older People (single copy) | May–Aug 2025 | £5.75 | | |

| POSTAGE AND PACKING CHARGES | | | | |
|---|---|---|---|---|
| Order value | UK | Europe | Rest of world | |
| Under £7.00 | £2.00 | | | |
| £7.00–£29.99 | £3.00 | Available on request | Available on request | |
| £30.00 and over | FREE | | | |

| | |
|---|---|
| Total value of books | |
| Donation* | |
| Postage and packing | |
| **Total for this order** | |

**Please complete in BLOCK CAPITALS**

*Please complete the Gift Aid declaration below

Title ............ First name/initials ...................... Surname ...........................................................

Address ...........................................................................................................................................

........................................................................................ Postcode .............................

Acc. No. ........................................ Telephone ..........................................................................

Email ...............................................................................................................................................

## Method of payment

❏ Cheque (made payable to BRF) ❏ MasterCard / Visa

Card no. ☐☐☐☐ ☐☐☐☐ ☐☐☐☐ ☐☐☐☐

Expires end ☐M☐M ☐Y☐Y Security code ☐☐☐ Last 3 digits on the reverse of the card

## BRF Ministries Gift Aid Declaration

In order to Gift Aid your donations, you must tick the box below.

*giftaid it*

❏ I want to Gift Aid my donation and any donation I make in the future or have made in the past four years to BRF Ministries.

I am a UK taxpayer and understand that if I pay less Income Tax and/or Capital Gains Tax in the current tax year than the amount of Gift Aid claimed on all my donations, it is my responsibility to pay any difference. Please notify BRF Ministries if you want to cancel this declaration, change your name or home address, or no longer pay sufficient tax on your income and/or capital gains.

**Please return this form to:**
BRF Ministries, 15 The Chambers, Vineyard,
Abingdon OX14 3FE | **enquiries@brf.org.uk**
For terms and cancellation information, please
visit **brfonline.org.uk/terms**.

We will use your personal data to process this order.
From time to time we may send you information
about the work of BRF Ministries. Please contact
us if you wish to discuss your mailing preferences
**brf.org.uk/privacy**

BROP0125

## BIBLE REFLECTIONS FOR OLDER PEOPLE **GROUP SUBSCRIPTION FORM**

All our Bible reading notes can be ordered online
by visiting **brfonline.org.uk/subscriptions**

The group subscription rate for *Bible Reflections for Older People* will be £17.25 per person until April 2026.

☐ I would like to take out a group subscription for ............ (*quantity*) copies.

☐ Please start my order with the May 2025 / September 2025 / January 2026* issue.
(*delete as appropriate*)

Please do not send any money with your order. Send your order to BRF Ministries and we will send you an invoice.

**Name and address of the person organising the group subscription:**

Title ............ First name/initials ....................... Surname......................................

Address.....................................................................................................

................................................................. Postcode ...........................

Telephone............................... Email................................................

Church...........................................................................................

**Name and address of the person paying the invoice if the invoice needs to be sent directly to them:**

Title ............ First name/initials ....................... Surname......................................

Address.....................................................................................................

................................................................. Postcode ...........................

Telephone............................... Email................................................

**Please return this form to:**
BRF Ministries, 15 The Chambers, Vineyard, Abingdon OX14 3FE | **enquiries@brf.org.uk**
For terms and cancellation information, please visit **brfonline.org.uk/terms**.

Bible Reading Fellowship is a charity (233280) and company limited by guarantee (301324), registered in England and Wales

BROP0125

## BIBLE REFLECTIONS FOR OLDER PEOPLE **INDIVIDUAL/GIFT SUBSCRIPTION FORM**

> To order online or set up a recurring subscription, visit **brfonline.org.uk/subscriptions**

☐ I would like to take out a subscription (*complete your name and address details only once*)
☐ I would like to give a gift subscription (*please provide both names and addresses*)

Title ............ First name/initials ......................... Surname...............................................

Address.....................................................................................................................

.................................................................................... Postcode ...............................

Telephone................................ Email................................................................

Gift subscription name .................................................................................................

Gift subscription address ..............................................................................................

.................................................................................... Postcode ...............................

Gift message (*20 words max. or include your own gift card*):

...............................................................................................................................

...............................................................................................................................

Please send *Bible Reflections for Older People* beginning with the May 2025 / September 2025 / January 2026* issue (*\*delete as appropriate*):

| (*please tick box*) | UK | Europe | Rest of world |
|---|---|---|---|
| ***Bible Reflections for Older People*** | ☐ £22.80 | ☐ £30.75 | ☐ £37.05 |

Total enclosed £ ..................... (*cheques should be made payable to 'BRF'*)

Please charge my MasterCard / Visa with £ .......................

Card no. ☐☐☐☐ ☐☐☐☐ ☐☐☐☐ ☐☐☐☐

Expires end ☐☐☐☐   Security code ☐☐   Last 3 digits on the reverse of the card

We will use your personal data to process this order. From time to time we may send you information about the work of BRF Ministries. Please contact us if you wish to discuss your mailing preferences **brf.org.uk/privacy.**

**Please return this form to:**
BRF Ministries, 15 The Chambers, Vineyard, Abingdon OX14 3FE | **enquiries@brf.org.uk**
For terms and cancellation information, please visit **brfonline.org.uk/terms.**

Bible Reading Fellowship is a charity (233280) and company limited by guarantee (301324), registered in England and Wales